X-SPORTS

SKELETON:
HIGH-SPEED ICE SLIDING

BY KIM COVERT

CONSULTANT:
KEN DELONG
FIBT INTERNATIONAL JUDGE

Capstone
press

Mankato, Minnesota

Edge Books are published by Capstone Press,
151 Good Counsel Drive, P.O. Box 669, Mankato, Minnesota 56002.
www.capstonepress.com

Library of Congress Cataloging-in-Publication Data
Covert, Kim.
    Skeleton : high-speed ice sliding / by Kim Covert.
    p. cm. -- (Edge books. X-sports)
    Includes bibliographical references and index.
    ISBN 0-7368-3784-1 (hardcover)
    1. Tobogganing--Juvenile literature. I. Title. II. Series.
GV856.C68 2005
796.95--dc22   2004021599

Summary: Introduces the sport of skeleton, including history, equipment, and famous
skeleton athletes.

Editorial Credits

Connie Colwell Miller, editor; Jason Knudson, set designer; Enoch Peterson and
    Linda Clavel, book designers; Jason D. Miller, illustrator; Jo Miller, photo
    researcher; Scott Thoms, photo editor

Photo Credits

Corbis/Duomo, 29; Duomo/Chris Trotman, 7, 13 (bottom), 15, 28; Reuters/
    Petar Kujundzic, 19
Getty Images Inc./AFP Photo/Arno Balzarini, 11; AFP Photo/George Frey, 13 (top), 16;
    Central Press, 9; Clive Mason, 27; Keystone/Chris Ware, 8; Robert Laberge, 5, 21;
    Shaun Botterill, cover
SportsChrome Inc./Bongarts/Sandra Behne, 17; Rob Tringali, 25

1 2 3 4 5 6 10 09 08 07 06 05

TABLE OF CONTENTS

Penworthy 5/05

CHAPTER 1

SKELETON

Jim Shea Jr. stands at the top of the Utah Olympic Park track. A green light flashes. Shea bends over and quickly pushes his sled toward the icy track. He leaps onto the sled and lies on his stomach. His arms are at his sides. Soon, he is speeding at almost 80 miles (129 kilometers) per hour down the track. His face is less than one-half inch (about 16 millimeters) from the ice.

Shea uses his body to control the sled. He makes small movements with his shoulders and legs to steer. Shea must travel through 15 curves in the track. He tries to find the fastest way through these turns.

LEARN ABOUT:

- The Cresta Run
- The 1928 Olympics
- Skeleton today

Jim Shea Jr.'s face nearly touches the ice as he races down the skeleton track.

At the bottom of the track, 15,000 fans watch as Shea crosses the finish line. He raced down the 4,397-foot (1,340-meter) track in 50.8 seconds. Shea wins the gold medal for the United States.

SKELETON HISTORY

Skeleton is one of the world's first sliding sports. It began in the 1880s in St. Moritz, Switzerland. In 1884, tourists helped build an icy track along a road from St. Moritz to the town of Celerina. They named this track the Cresta Run. Racers rode wooden sleds down the Cresta Run.

Around 1887, racers began lying down on the sleds headfirst. The sleds went much faster down the track this way. By 1890, all Cresta Run racers rode headfirst.

In 1889, racers began using sleds made of metal. Some people thought the sleds looked like human skeletons. Many people believe that this sled is how the sport got its name. The sport's name might also come from the word *schlitten*. This word means "sled" in German.

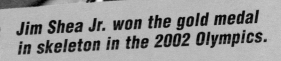

Jim Shea Jr. won the gold medal in skeleton in the 2002 Olympics.

AN OLYMPIC EVENT

Skeleton races were held at the Winter Olympics for the first time in 1928. The Games were held in St. Moritz. Fifteen men from six countries raced in the skeleton event.

In 1948, skeleton was part of the Olympics again, also at St. Moritz. After the 1948 Games, skeleton was not part of the Olympics for many years. Many people thought skeleton racing was too dangerous.

In the 1970s, skeleton became popular again in Europe. International competitions began in 1987. Athletes from 20 countries competed in the 1992 World Cup series.

The first Olympic skeleton races were held in St. Moritz, Switzerland.

The first skeleton sleds were made of wood or metal.

2002 OLYMPICS

Skeleton returned to the Olympics in 2002. Skeleton teams from 30 countries came to Salt Lake City, Utah. Women competed in the event for the first time.

Today, skeleton continues to become more popular. Many countries have skeleton programs. The U.S. Bobsled and Skeleton Federation has a junior skeleton school for high school students. Athletes like the excitement of speeding down the track headfirst at high speeds.

CHAPTER 2

SKELETON GEAR

Skeleton athletes need equipment that helps prevent injuries. They must wear helmets with a chin guard. They wear goggles or face shields to protect their eyes and face. Sliders also wear gloves. Some sliders wear elbow, shoulder, and knee pads under or over their suits. The pads protect the sliders when they bump the sides of the track.

Sliders want to go as fast as possible. They wear tight bodysuits made of a stretchy material. This clothing does not slow down the sleds. Sliders also wear shoes with spikes on the bottom. The spikes grip the ice when the sliders push off at the start.

LEARN ABOUT:
- Safety gear
- Sleds and runners
- Ballast

Sliders wear helmets, gloves, face shields, and bodysuits.

SKELETON SLEDS

Skeleton sleds are made of steel and fiberglass. The sleds have no steering devices. Sleds must be between 31 and 47 inches (80 and 120 centimeters) long.

Two stainless steel runners attach to the bottom of each sled. The runners are about 1 inch (2.5 centimeters) wide. Racers polish the runners to help the sleds go faster.

The sleds have weight requirements. Men's sleds can't weigh more than 72.8 pounds (33 kilograms). Women's sleds must weigh 63.9 pounds (29 kilograms) or less. The total weight of the sled and athlete can't be more than 253.5 pounds (115 kilograms) for men. For women, the total weight must be less than 202.8 pounds (92 kilograms).

Sliders can add ballast to their sleds up to the weight limits. This weight helps the sleds travel faster. Sliders are not allowed to add ballast to their bodies.

Today's skeleton sleds are made of steel and fiberglass.

Stainless steel runners allow sleds to glide across the ice.

CHAPTER 3

STRATEGY AND COMPETITIONS

Skeleton racers travel down the track as quickly as possible. Skeleton racers must practice their starts and their runs to succeed at the sport.

THE START

Skeleton racers need a fast start. The racers push their sleds for up to 55 yards (50 meters) at the top of the track. They usually cover this distance in about five seconds. Then, they dive smoothly onto the sled.

Sliders train all year to stay in shape. They lift weights to build their muscles. Sliders also do sprint training. This training helps them run fast while pushing their heavy sleds.

LEARN ABOUT:

- A fast start
- The skeleton track
- Competing in skeleton

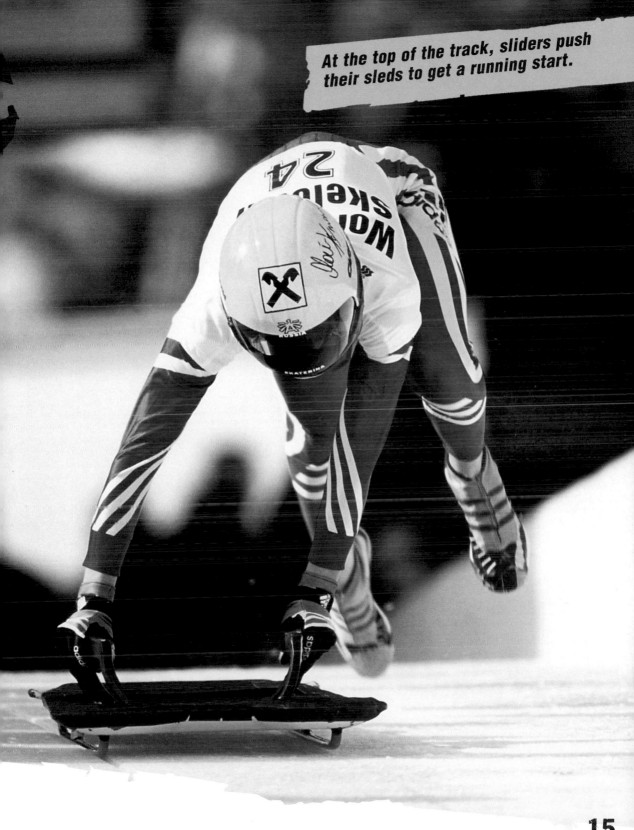

At the top of the track, sliders push their sleds to get a running start.

Sliders quickly dive onto their sleds and begin to speed down the track.

THE RUN

Before a race, sliders study all the curves on the track. They want to find the fastest way through each turn. Many athletes go through the track in their minds dozens of times before a run.

The slider's starting push powers the sled. Then, the pull of gravity helps the slider speed between 70 and 80 miles (113 and 129 kilometers) per hour. This speed is faster than cars travel on most highways.

The sliders can feel up to five g-forces (Gs) while racing. At five Gs, they feel up to five times heavier than usual. Space shuttle astronauts feel five Gs when the shuttle launches. Sliders build strong neck muscles to handle the high Gs in the curves.

Sliders keep their eyes on the course during the entire run.

Skeleton sliders must concentrate to avoid injuries. The high Gs can cause their faces to smash into the ice at the turns. Sometimes, their chin guards wear a groove into the icy track. Sliders can bruise themselves or break bones by bumping into the icy walls. They might get cuts and scrapes if they fall off their sleds.

Skeleton sleds do not have brakes. Sliders use their feet to stop after they reach the finish line. Some tracks have foam pads or snow at the end of the track to help sliders stop.

EDGE FACT

Before each race, officials check to make sure the runners are not heated. Heated runners slide over the ice more easily. This would be unfair to other sliders.

Skeleton sliders travel so fast that they feel up to five times heavier than usual.

COMPETITIONS

In 1923, the Federation Internationale de Bobsleigh et de Tobagganing (FIBT) was formed. The FIBT sets rules for skeleton racing. It also organizes championships for amateur sliders around the world. These championships include the World Cup Tour, the World Championships, and the Junior World Championships.

The World Cup is a series of contests held during the winter at tracks around the world. World Cup contestants compete in two races, or heats, in one day. The slider with the lowest of the two combined heat times wins.

World Championship sliders compete in four heats over two days. The winner has the lowest of the four combined heat times.

Developing athletes have their own competitions. The America Cup and European Cup are races for these sliders. Athletes under age 22 can compete in the Junior World Championships. Many countries have programs for beginners to learn skeleton racing.

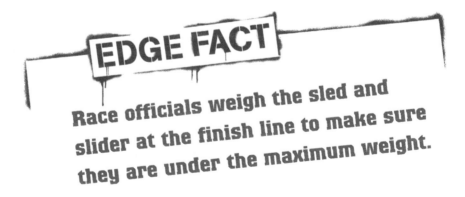

EDGE FACT

Race officials weigh the sled and slider at the finish line to make sure they are under the maximum weight.

Skeleton sliders must stay focused to avoid injuries at such high speeds.

THE START!

1. The slider runs on the icy track while holding the handles of the sled.

2. Still running, the slider dives onto the sled. Sometimes, a slider's feet fly high in the air while jumping on the sled.

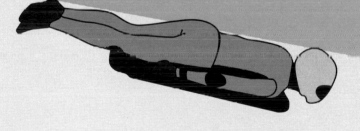

3. The slider lies facedown.
   Tucking both arms close
   to the body, the slider
   grips the handles of
   the sled.

CHAPTER 4

SKELETON ATHLETES

Many skeleton racers began racing bobsleds or a type of sled called a luge. They soon found they liked the thrill of speeding down tracks headfirst on skeleton sleds. These athletes helped skeleton become more popular around the world.

JIM SHEA JR.

Jim Shea Jr. raced bobsleds before trying skeleton. He was scared after his first skeleton run. But he wanted to do it again right away. He thought it was more exciting than bobsledding. Shea made the U.S. skeleton team in 1995. In 1999, he became the skeleton World Champion. In 2002, he qualified for the Olympics.

LEARN ABOUT:

- Tristan Gale
- Jeff Pain
- Michelle Kelly

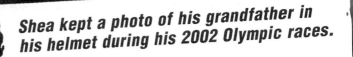

Shea kept a photo of his grandfather in his helmet during his 2002 Olympic races.

SALT LAKE 2002

Shea was the third member of his family to compete in the Winter Olympics. His father raced in three cross-country ski events in the 1964 Olympics. His grandfather won two speed skating medals at the 1932 Olympics. Shea's grandfather died in a car crash a few weeks before the 2002 Olympics. Shea kept a picture of his grandfather in his helmet during his Olympic races.

TRISTAN GALE

In 2002, Tristan Gale became the first Olympic women's skeleton champion. Gale started in winter sports as a downhill skier. Her family moved to Salt Lake City, Utah, when she was a teenager. She learned about skeleton at a bobsled tryout and started competing in the sport in 1998.

Gale competed on the World Cup circuit for the first time during the 2001–2002 season. Her highest place was eighth in a World Cup event. Gale was 21 when she won the Olympic gold medal.

Tristan Gale was the first woman to win an Olympic gold medal in skeleton.

Gale finished the next season ranked third in the world among women. She won bronze medals at the World Championships and the Junior World Championships.

JEFF PAIN

Canadian Jeff Pain began as a bobsled athlete. He didn't do well, so he switched to the luge. In 1996, he tried skeleton. He liked the challenge of racing headfirst down the course.

Pain won the gold medal in the 2003 World Championships. He also placed second overall in the World Cup rankings.

Jeff Pain took first place in the 2003 World Championships.

Michelle Kelly is the first Canadian woman to win the World Championships.

MICHELLE KELLY

Michelle Kelly of Canada was a gymnast for 13 years. She began racing bobsled in 1994. The next year, she started training in skeleton. Kelly raced in both events for a few years. In 1999, she decided to focus on skeleton. She finished 10th at the 2002 Olympics.

In 2003, Kelly won the World Championships and the first-place ranking in the World Cup. Kelly is the first Canadian woman to win these titles.

Skeleton is still not a well-known sport. Today's sliders are helping the sport become more popular.

GLOSSARY

ballast (BAL-uhst)—heavy material that adds weight to make a sled go faster

bobsled (BOB-sled)—a sled with a steering mechanism and brakes for racing down an icy track

fiberglass (FYE-bur-glass)—a strong, lightweight material made from woven threads of glass

g-force (GEE-forss)—a feeling of increased weight caused by traveling very fast

gravity (GRAV-uh-tee)—the force that pulls people and objects down toward the earth

heat (HEET)—a single run down the skeleton course in a competition

luge (LOOZH)—a one- or two-person sled used for racing down a track; athletes ride a luge feet-first on their backs.

READ MORE

Wallechinsky, David. *The Complete Book of the Winter Olympics.* Woodstock, N.Y.: Overlook Press, 2001.

Wukovits, John F. *The Encyclopedia of the Winter Olympics.* New York: Franklin Watts, 2001.

INTERNET SITES

FactHound offers a safe, fun way to find Internet sites related to this book. All of the sites on FactHound have been researched by our staff.

Here's how:

1. Visit *www.facthound.com*
2. Type in this special code **0736837841** for age-appropriate sites. Or enter a search word related to this book for a more general search.
3. Click on the **Fetch It** button.

FactHound will fetch the best sites for you!

INDEX